Simple Life Poetry

Martin D. White

PublishAmerica
Baltimore

© 2007 by Martin D. White.
All rights reserved. No part of this book may be reproduced, stored in a retrieval system or transmitted in any form or by any means without the prior written permission of the publishers, except by a reviewer who may quote brief passages in a review to be printed in a newspaper, magazine or journal.

First printing

ISBN: 1-4241-1913-8
PUBLISHED BY PUBLISHAMERICA, LLLP
www.publishamerica.com
Baltimore

Printed in the United States of America

Welcome to *Simple Life Poetry*.
A collection of poems
Written by
Martin D. White
Author of
Living the Simple Life

www.livingthesimplelife.com

Dedicated to

My wife
Whose love inspires me to write.

And all the members of my
Poetry Forum
www.poetstage.com

A place for poets to share.

My Philosophy

I consider myself a writer that occasionally writes poetry;
Unlike true poets on poetstage.com I do see;
I see myself as different, than most people you see;
To know what I mean you must understand my philosophy;
To start with, feel your emotions but make them behave;
If you don't, you will end up being their slave;
Make friends with your anger, which will be a chore;
Once you do, you will find, there will be no reason to get mad anymore;
When angry people come to you, it is compassion they need;
Instead of getting angry, compassion you feed;
Spend your day giving to each person you meet;
Because every bit caring you give, comes back to you complete;
Reality is just an illusion, is what I got to say;
It is only that you believe it, that makes it that way;
If you truly believe you are happy, then happy you will be;
And you will start to see things with my philosophy.

Writing Poetry

When I write poems I get to say;
Things from my heart expressed a different way;
Poetry allows me to express just how I feel;
It unlocks my heart and makes me feel real;
Thoughts in my mind sometimes are a total mess;
Saying it in poetry allows me to express;
It allows me to express my feelings, using what rhymes;
In such a way that you know the feelings from between the lines;
When life gets me down and answers are hard to see;
I can find the answers to my problems when I write poetry.

Life

In order to tell you about a day in the life of me;
You have to take time to learn a new philosophy;
There is a lot of Negativity in the world today;
It is impossible to stay positive some people will say;
Some days things just go wrong no matter what you do;
Whether you have a good day or bad is still up to you;
Some days it seem problems, just won't go away;
These are just problems happening in the course of a great day;
Good days and bad are not determined by
what is before your eyes;
Good days and bad days in your head it does lie;
Most people will say reality is a bunch of shit;
I think reality is just a fantasy unless you really believe it.

Simple Life Poetry
Author
Martin D. White

www.livingthesimplelife.com

Life Is a Beach

I always did call the ocean my home;
Because my heart is always there, no matter where I Roam;

When I am at the ocean, I hear the crashing of the wave;
It brings me back to center, and my sanity it does save;
Looking out into the ocean and the vastness of it all;
You realize in comparison, this country is pretty small;
Living in Indiana surrounded by corn;
I know my heart is broken, always in a state of torn;
A sunrise over the ocean is something you should see;
I can't believe it happens every morning without me;
When I start to think about it, it brings me to a tear;
Knowing that I cannot be down there for another year;
When I am at the ocean my heart does it teach;
That's why I always say, life is a beach.

Unconscious State

Every one of us is walking around in an unconscious state;
Being controlled by our emotions, determines our fate;
Little do we know that we all have the key;
To unlock our emotions and set them free;
In everyone's mind there is a giant wall;
This wall is full of light switches, our emotions in all;
All of our switches are on, good ones and bad;
Love, hate, depression, happiness and sad;
I have a little secret I would like to share with you;
To be happy in life, shut off the bad ones,
is all you have to do;
Once you shut off anger off, it will stay;
Until you walk over and let it come out to play;
Anger needs to stay off, from what I can see;
It will destroy your life and is a waste of electricity;
Once you shut off anger, it will give you a fit;
Make friends with your anger to understand it;
You must learn to feel every emotion,
in each and every room;Feel your emotions, but your life it must not consume;
Always put out good energy no matter what you do;
The kind of energy you put out is what comes back to you;
When problems get you down and your emotions seem so large;
Remember you control the light switches,
and the emotions will not be in charge.

My First Kiss

I was the age of five, just a little boy
When my little sister had over a friend, and her name was Joy;
I remember they played Barbies for just a little while;
And I of course was Super Man with my cape of towel;
After a while of bugging them they finally let me play;
I became the astronaut all the rest of the day;
I flew out in my space ship to save the planet of two;
No matter how many enemies, because victory I knew;
With my space ship and I not one did I miss;
Why, because every time I returned home,
I got a hero's kiss.

Silhouette

(Adult Theme)

She stands in the corner for everyone to see;
Someone that God has made just for me;

In a poorly lit room I see her silhouette;
Once she caught my eye everything else I forget;

Each soft round curve calls to my desire;
A single touch from her sets me on fire;

Each curve I crave to taste from bottom to top;
Working slowly back down to the middle, where I
Cannot stop;

Creating an unending appetite that comes in quite handy;
Like a little boy in a store with a bag full of candy;

With each taste I crave more and I want to stay;
Until she stops counting the number of times,
And pushes me away.

Where I sit, patiently waiting for her energy to restore;
With nothing on my mind but the craving for more;

I stand in the corner waiting over by a wall;
Hypnotized by her silhouette, at her beck and call.

Lost Love

After too many years in a marriage full of hate;
I managed to break free before it was too late;

Living every day in a marriage without any love;
Makes you feel like the sky,
will come crashing down from above;

A short time after I was set free;
I met a girl I thought loved me;

For once in my life I could actually say;
I was in love every single day;

Friendship and my heart did I share;
Not knowing behind my back, was something in the air;

I loved her so deep, and it is hard to say;
How I felt when she moved in with another guy,
on Valentine's Day.

Hair

When I was young, I was happy every day;
Care free and young I used to play;
Then came the day that would forever change my life;
The event was so horrible I could not tell my wife;
It was the day that my life as I know it, came to a screeching stop;
I sank into depression and my bubble did pop;
I did not know if I could face the next day;
Thinking that God would come down and take me away;
I could not talk to people and look them in the eye;
I know my time was short and soon would I die;
Thoughts came to my mind of ending my life now;
Because going on with life, I could not see how;
You might wonder what kind of event
would cause such despair;
It was the day I found out I was losing my hair.

Clocks

I remember when I was little and going to my grandparents' house;
I would sit in their living room, where it was quiet as a mouse;
My grandpa owned four grandfather clocks and over me they tower;
I would sit in that living room waiting for the top of the hour;
I knew that when the hand hit twelve even before I knew how to tell time;
That all four grandfather clocks, would play wind mister chime;
When all of them played the sound was quite so grand;
Every top of the hour in that living room I would stand;
Now that I am an adult, hanging on my wall;
I have a clock that every hour takes me back
to when I was small.

Hot Wheels

From as far back as I can remember one toy had appeal;
I had a big collection, and I loved my hot wheels;
I would play with them every night and up late I would stay; When my mom fell asleep, she would become the highway;
I remember they bought me a city and for hours would I play;
I remember I had a cop car and speeders, they would pay;
Other times I was the speeder running from the cop;
I would always lose them by pulling into my shop;
Sometimes I was a dad taking the kids for a ride;
Not knowing where I was going, I let the kids decide;
When I got a little older my parents bought me a track;
I always was the winner because challengers speed they did lack;
Even until my early teens for hours I would drive;
Having hundreds of horrible crashes, but always would survive;
Now that I am an adult and even my car has a loan;
I still remember the day when all the roads I did own.

Rhyming

I have a small problem with writing with Rhyme;
Once I get started, I do it all the time;
I write the first sentence as easy as can be;
But for some reason the second line just comes to me;
I tried to see a doctor and tell him I am ill;
He laughed me out of his office and gave to me a pill;
Always writing letters to my boss, with a little twist;
Even memos to myself, and my grocery list;
I need to face my illness and learn to control;
Before it becomes too bad and takes away my soul;
Someone must free me from this hell of mine;
Because every second sentence always must, (you know);
It is mind over matter, some people will say;
Well my mind is stuck on this matter and is going to stay;Maybe there is a group out there, that will help me quit;
Or maybe there is a doctor to help me stop this poop.

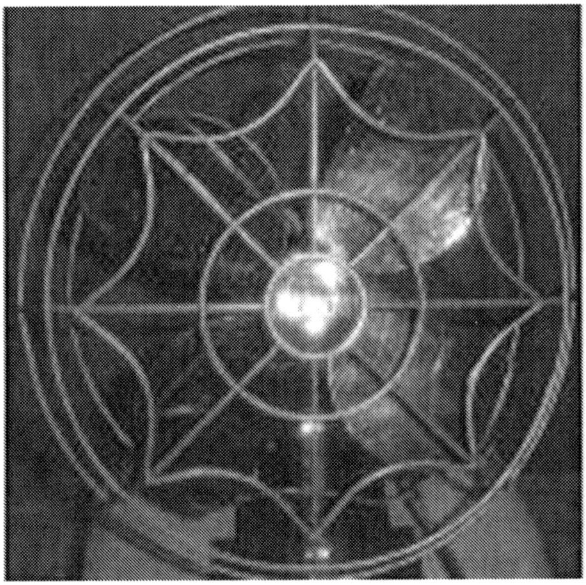

Fran the Fan

I am writing this poem about someone very close to me;
Her and I are inseparable when there is no AC;
With her shiny black blades and her bright chrome middle;
I am captivated by her beauty and for which I can do little;
When the weather is hot, she is always by my side;Pleasuring me fast or slow, whichever I decide;

In stationary mode our love has no ends;
In oscillating mode she will pleasure my friends;
With her fast quiet motor, made by a man;
The name of my love is "Fran," my Fan.

Royalty

Living with royalty is such a big to-do;
Catering to her every whim, I have worn a hole in my shoe;
With the cars in the yard and the halter tops on the line;
She spends from morning to night, sipping on fine wine;
Her bed is made of fine linens, shipped in from the world's far part;
Bought only at the finest stores including Kmart;
She has the face of an Actress, Usually found riding brooms;
Her body is a temple, that could use to shed a few rooms;

Her faithfulness to me cannot be bought;
She gives it away for free, to anyone who sought;

She spends her days in the stores,
buying like money grows on a tree;
Buying jewelry and clothes or anything marked
"AS SEEN ON TV"
You might wonder what kind of royalty makes the hounds bark;
Well the royalty I am married to is the
Queen of the Trailer park.

Searching

I have lost something that is very dear to me;
I have looked high and low and cannot see;
I had it when I was young it made me feel good;
I ask all my friends, they say they would help me if they could;
I lost it more than twenty years ago and it seems so far;
Maybe I left it in the back seat of some car;
I've looked in my home town, I've looked in my house;
I have asked my mom and dad and even my spouse;
I've checked in my wallet, and under my bed;
I even had a séance so I can ask the dead;
I've cleaned out my closet, and my storage bin;
The fact that I lost it, seems quite a sin;
I have looked for so long, in this task I must not taper;
I even ran an advertisement in the local newspaper;
You might wonder what I have lost that is so dear to me;
Well, what I have lost is my virginity.

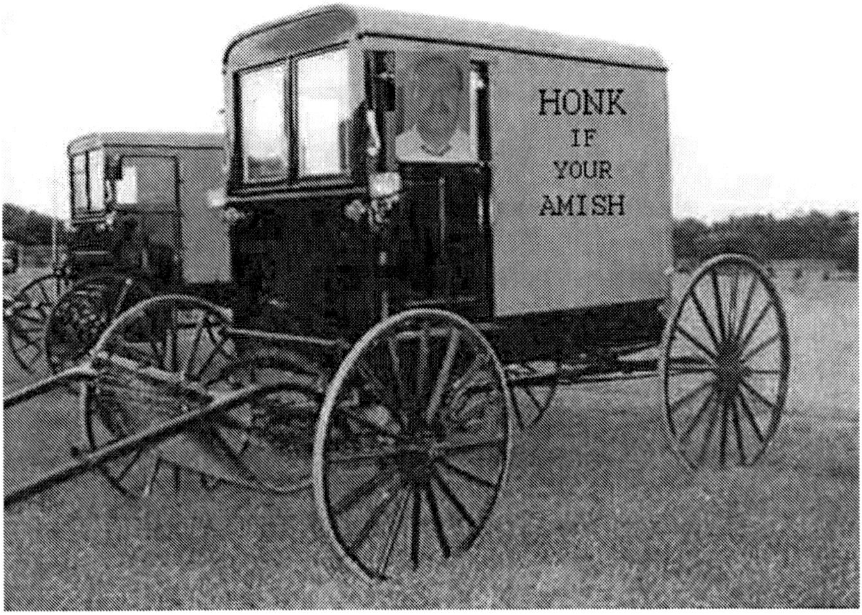
HONK
IF
YOUR
AMISH

The Amish Life

I get up in the morning before the sun, it does rise;
Stumbling in the dark because I can't see anything before my eyes;

Making it to the kitchen, a candle I do light;Needing a cup of coffee with not a coffee maker in sight;
Facing a hard day of chores is what I do see;
Well, it's not like I am going to sit around and watch TV;
Planting dur fields and running dur farm;
Always asking God, would a tractor be such a harm;
Hitching up the buggy, everywhere seems so far;
Wondering, if God really would hate me, if I owned a car;
Instead, I have to find Mennonites, who souls are for sell;
I get to ride in a car, and they get to burn in hell;
Always dressed in black, might help me look thin;
Thinking, why would having a little color be such a sin;
At night I go to bed with my wife,
but I don't know what for;
With five layers of clothes, to keep warm,
sex is a chore;
As most of you reading this, surely can see;
I am having a little doubt, dur Amish life is for me.

Winter

Winter is a season I don't really like;
I would rather see summer and me on a hike;

Snow and Ice on the ground, every winter since I was a lass;
Wearing five layers of clothes and still freezing my butt;

Everything from freezing your face by taking out the trash;
To driving your car on icy roads, hoping you do not crash;

I have friends, who have snow mobiles and go Ice Fishing;
They would be at the bottom of that lake, if I had what I was wishing;

Everywhere around you, icicles they do form;
And days in the 30s seems, really warm;

In the Hot warm sun, I do want to Baska;
People who like winter, should move to Alaska;

Spending every day in the cold, freezing to the bone;
Thinking a winter place down south, is what I should own;

Getting home everyday and the layers you start peeling;
Hoping that maybe someday your hand, will regain its feeling;

Once you have driven to work following a salt truck;
You have seen the truth, that *Winters really do suck.*

Santa

Once a year I would sit down and write him a letter;
Confessing all my sins and promising to do better;
I would make a nice list, and tell him what to bring;
Each year from my list, was not a single thing;
When I saw what he brought me, it always made me laugh;
Elves might be good toy builders, but make really crappy office staff;
I know their work load is big and it is hard to keep up with the pace;
I assume I am on some computer with a large Database.
Each year I would send a follow-up letter
and the mistake I would show;
I figured it was a cross-reference problem, most likely a typo;
One year I sent a letter to help him with his mess;
I told him instead of hand delivery try UPS;
The following year I waited on UPS and my house they did miss;
I guess if you complain too much,
you automatically make the Naughty list;
Each year I sent a letter for them to ignore;
So what if I am an adult, age 44;
I write out my letter and in the envelope do I pack;
I guess once on the Naughty List, there is no going back;
At first of December my life I do pause;
So I can write my letter starting with Dear Santa Claus.

Never Been Kissed

When two lips touch for the very first time;
Both Hearts stop, and you hear a chime;
With the nerviness of the moment
and the excitement of it all;
It is like not paying attention and walking into a wall;
You walk around like a zombie for the next several days;
Dumbfounded by the moment in total amaze;
Now that you know what is like to have a very first kiss;
Grab the cutest person around you
and
make sure you don't miss.

You Choose

After living many years in a marriage without love;
I was given a gift from the man up above;
We started off as friends with one simple date;
Little did I know it was going to determine my fate;
Get involved with someone younger, no way she did say.
After that first date we knew we would wed someday;
When two hearts connect from the very start;
You do not feel whole when you are apart;
An answer to my prayers he did send;
Not only find a lover but, a very best friend;
Connecting every day, through good times and bad;
Supporting each other through happiness and sad;
To have someone to spend with the rest of my life;

Romantic or Funny you pick the ending:

1. Someone I can proudly call my wife;
2. But, please don' t tell my wife

Toad

At a high school dance on the other side of the room;
A spotlight beamed on her,
and my heart she did consume; With her long blonde hair and cute little smile;
I was like a deer caught in the headlights,
for quite a while;

Maybe I should talk to her
Maybe we should dance;
Maybe she would talk to me;
Maybe I would have a chance;
Maybe she would look at me with Love in her eyes;
Maybe she would realize without me she would die;

Together, maybe we can drive down that lovers' road;
Oh wait I can't, because,
I am but a toad.

Smells

In everywhere you go and no matter what you do;
There is a brand-new world right in front of you;
It is always around you, and might come to quite a surprise;
To see this brand-new world, you have to shut your eyes;
This brand-new world is always with you,
no matter where you go;
Breathe in deep through your nose and it will begin to show;
Everywhere you are, you will feel a brand-new force;
Always breathe it in deep, except for the bathroom of course;
You will see things you cannot see,
right before your eyes;
As if your other senses,
were telling you big fat lies;
While smelling is very important, and I wish to give it its due;
I just thank God, people don't greet people, the way doggies do.

Frying Pan

I am lying on the floor dizzy, and really can't tell you why;
I see stars in front of me but they are not up in the sky;
I was having a great day, talking to my wife;
We was talking about our love and our great life;

She ask me about my health, she ask me about my work
She ask me about my sister, and my brother-in-law the jerk.
She ask me about my father, she ask me about my mother.
She ask me about my aunt, she ask me about my brother;
She ask me to mow the lawn, she ask me to take out the trash;
She ask me to look at her arm, because she has some rash;
She ask me about her hair, she ask me about her shoe;
She ask me if her pants made her look fat, and I said,
Yes you bet they do.

So I am lying on the floor wondering who I am;
Next to me on the floor is a Frying Pan

Once in a Lifetime

Once in a Lifetime
Once in a lifetime, you will hear a chime;
When you meet someone special for the very first time.
Excitement is in the air and each moment you do feel;
You think you are in a fantasy but you know it is real;

Anticipating the next moment until you will be with;Someone that is real but seems like a myth;

From the moment our hearts touched,
a big part of mine stayed with you;
And when we were apart I felt empty and blue.

When I was away from you,
each hour seemed like days;
When I was with you, I was so happy;
I walked everywhere in total amaze;

From that very first connection
when we became one;
We have shared happiness and sadness together,
And as best friends, still had fun;

After Five years of being married feelings die down,
some people will say;

I just know I love you, even more than that very first day.
Love your Hubby

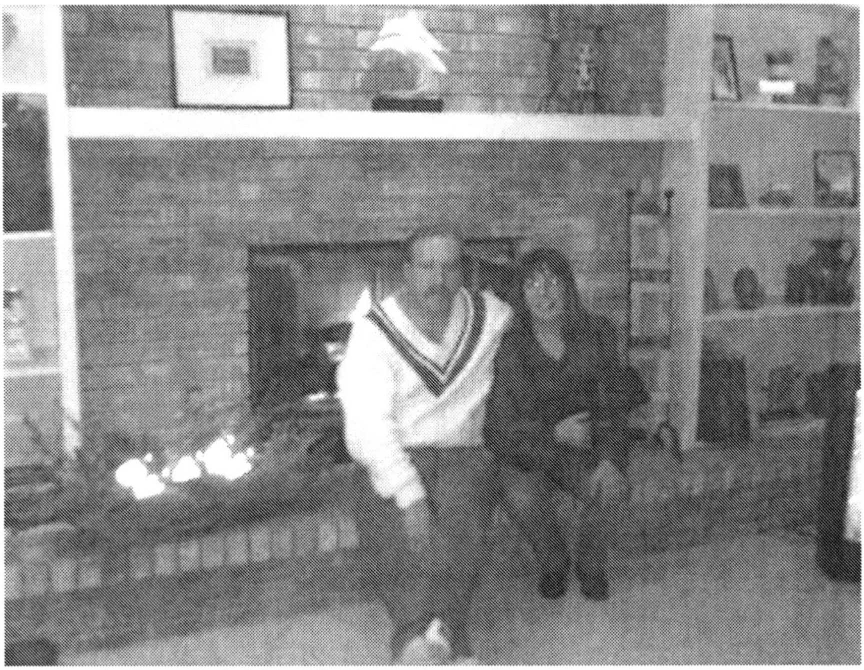

Husband & Wife

When two hearts come together as one;
They beat in time together under the sun;
Facing each day with the other's strength;
Longing for each other no matter what the length;
All the happiness and sadness they do fair;
Each victory and failure each night, do they share;
All good times and bad times they each face in part;
Keeping the love for each other deep in their heart.
Facing people with problems that never seem to end;
Knowing that each other, are each other's very best friend;
Each day is full of love and affection is a must;
Learning to open their hearts and give their trust;
Each problem that they face,
Each hurdle they must cross;
Each family member they gain,
Each family member loss;
Each heartache caused by others;
And even each other's mothers
During life's ups and downs, that might make them blue;
The one constant in their life is that the love for each other is true.

A Christmas Poem
for my Wife

Spending Christmas with you, is very
special to me;
Even in these hard times with not much
under the tree;
All the presents in the world I would not replace;
The love I feel every day,
when I see your face;
Each day is filled with presents,
Each moment with joy;
Each minute with happiness;
Each of us knowing, who is
my favorite toy;
Your love is with me every day in
everything that I do;
To me Christmas is every day because I have you!
Love
Your Hubby

A Valentine Poem
for my Wife

My wife is my best friend with whom I share my soul;
When we are together is when I feel whole;
Each day is filled with love from morning till night;
Each moment of the day I long to hold her tight;
She is my inspiration during a course of a hard day;
Coming home to her makes all pain and worry go away;
When we hug and kiss each other I do cherish;
Without her in my life each day I surely would perish;
Each moment in a day I share with you;
Each heartache and pain you help me pull through;
Through good times and bad we have each other;
Not only as a friend but also a lover.
On this Valentines in the year 2002;
I want you to know that I love you.

Your Husband

Sixth Wedding Anniversary Poem

I think there is something wrong with me, I think I am ill;
When I am around her all time just stands still;
I am frozen in time and my breath she does take;
Like ripples from a rock thrown into a lake;
Not a word comes out when I try to speak;
I start to feel lightheaded and my legs start getting weak;
It is hard to really explain just how I felt;
Only every time she looks at me, I start to melt;I spent our first date in a fog in some kind of a blur;
I tripped a couple times and spilled something on her;
Ever since that first date I have her on my mind;
Our date was a disaster and she was so kind;
I spent the whole night wondering if a second date I would see;
Well six years ago today, she married me.

A Poem for Patty

Expecting a First Child is a very special time in your life;
In a blink of a eye you go from Child to woman to wife;

As you get older you learn that life passes so fast;
During this special time make each moment last;

The love for your child is growing every day;
As she will grow, so will your love in a different way;

The time you share now, as you two are one;
You will always share this love through sad times and fun;

Children are a Blessing to each one of us;
Even on the days when they are late for the school bus;
A lesson in patience you are about to learn;
By the time you start to master it, it will be their turn;

So don't feel bad for the mistakes, you are about to make;
I mean they don't come with instructions for God's sake;

There will be presents you can't afford to buy;
because the budget it is above;
But that is ok,
Because the most important present you can give
is a big hug
and
all of your love.
Love;
Your Uncle Marty

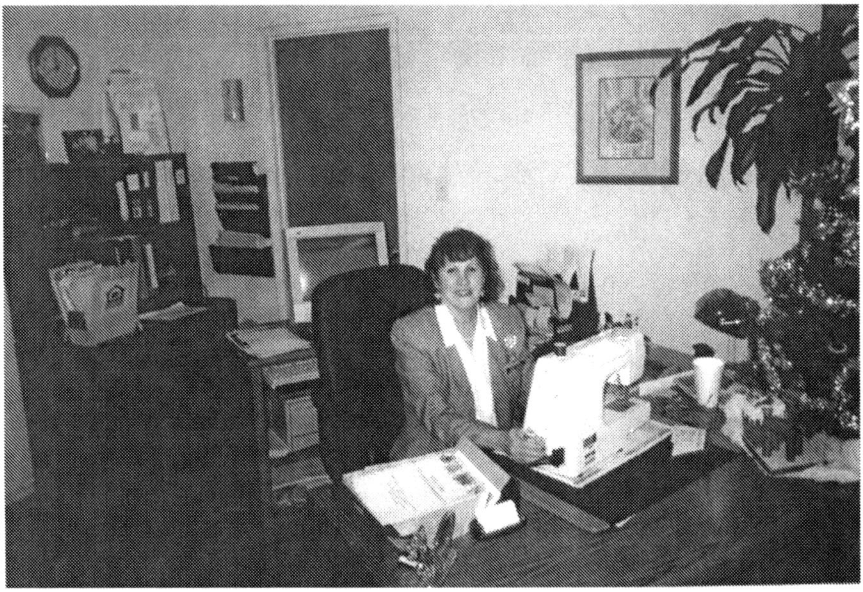

A Poem for My Mother

Your mother is someone that is always there for you;
She has gone from changing your diaper to tying your shoe;
Through boy scouts and baseball and even the flu;
Through your teens,
where she deserves a medal,
for just putting up with you;
From the time you are born, no matter how far away;
A little part of you, in her heart, you do stay;
Each achievement and failure in life you do share;
With a safety net of caring, you know she will be there;
For most of my grown life, many miles do we part;
But I never felt I really miss her because,
every day I have her with me in my heart;
Even when there are times;
That we do not agree;
I need to tell her how;
Very special she is to me;
During the course of my life I will love many others;
But none of them can replace the love for my mother.

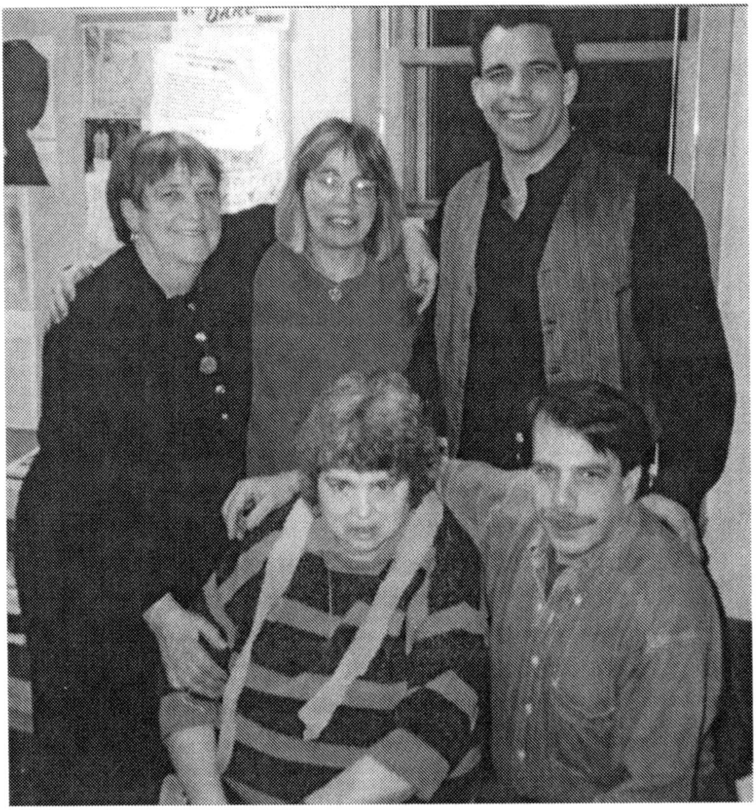

A Mothers-in-Law's Poem

When you enter into a family, even by marriage;
You show up with a horse and bright white carriage;
Living up to this image,
is something you hope to see;
Doing this is easy when I let myself be me;
Gaining a new mother is something very special to me;
Someone with a kind heart, which is easy to see;
When she is away, we miss her so very much;
Especially on Mother's Day, Christmas and such;
We hope she keeps in mind each and every day;
How much we love her in a very special way;
I say all this to you with my heart, my bones, and my joints;
Because frankly, I could use the Brownie Points.
Love Marty

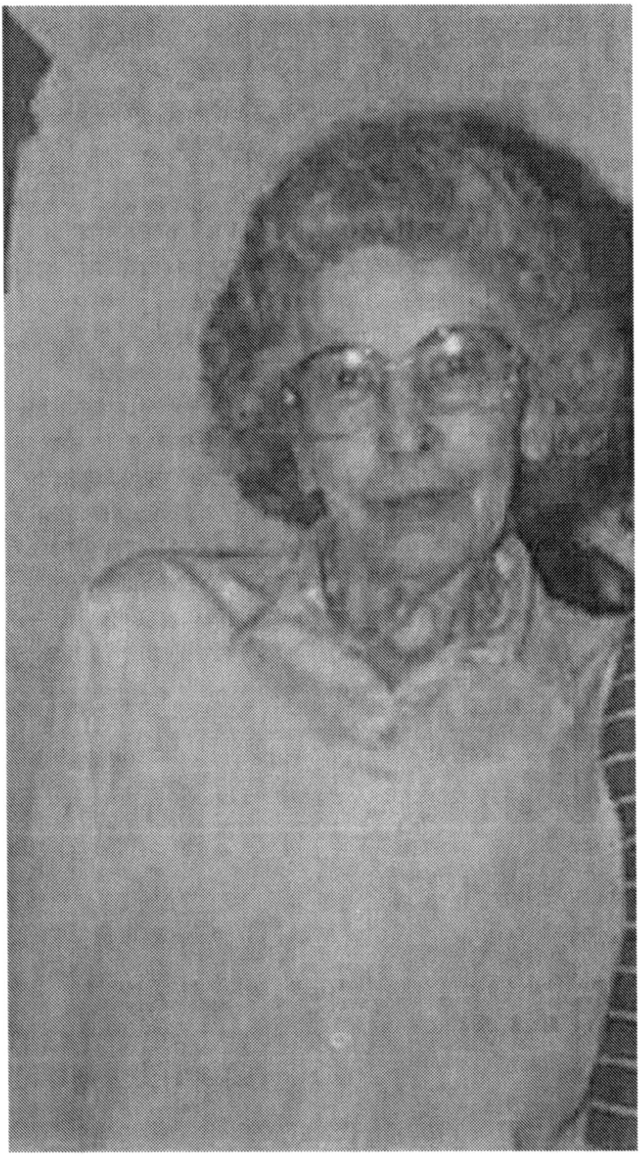

My Grandma

I remember the times when I was just a little boy;
Spending the weekend with my grandma and feeling lots of joy;
Doing things together and the joy it did bring;
Sharing many hobbies including bird watching;
To this day I can tell you most any bird I see;
Knowing most of the kinds of birds from what she taught me;
I remember evenings with TV dinners and watching TV;
Looking forward during the week for the next time,
she would be with me;
Working in the yard together and my labor she did hire;
Burning trash in the barrel, and even accidentally catching
a field on fire;In my late teens, out of state, I did move away;
But with my time I did spend, in my heart she did stay;
Toward the end of her life she stayed in a nursing home;
I went to visit weekly, no matter where I did roam;
We connected every week, and in her heart I won;
Even when she couldn't remember who I was and introduced
me as her son;
I had cherished every moment with her up to the day;
When I got the call she had passed away.

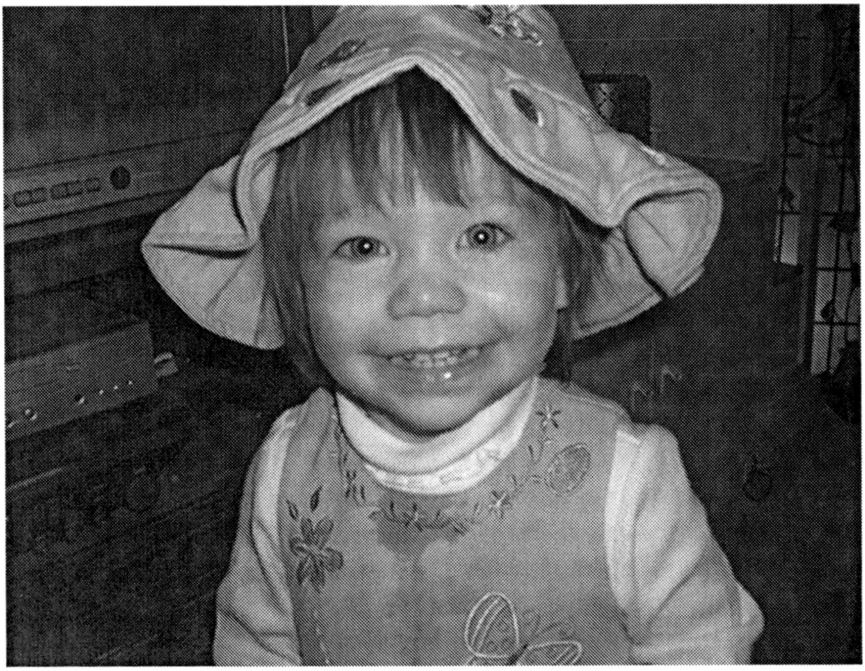

Smiley

Written for Eliza
My Granddaughter

There once was a Princess and it is easy to see;
Why she melts my heart each time she smiles at me;
The magic in her face, the questions in her eyes;
The giggles she does make and even her sighs;

The expressions she makes let you know you are there;
Holding tightly on your finger shows the love she does share;

A granddaughter is so special, the connection you can't explain;
A child of a child is twice the love you do gain.

Time away from her my heart is always torn;
because a lifetime of love was there, the minute she was born;

Our time with her is so special, and never seems like enough;
Looking forward to the next time sometimes is very tough;

Time seems a little empty, each time we are apart;But, looking at this picture allows me to put her back in my heart.

Looking forward to the future and things we are about to share;
Knowing that smiley will always be there.

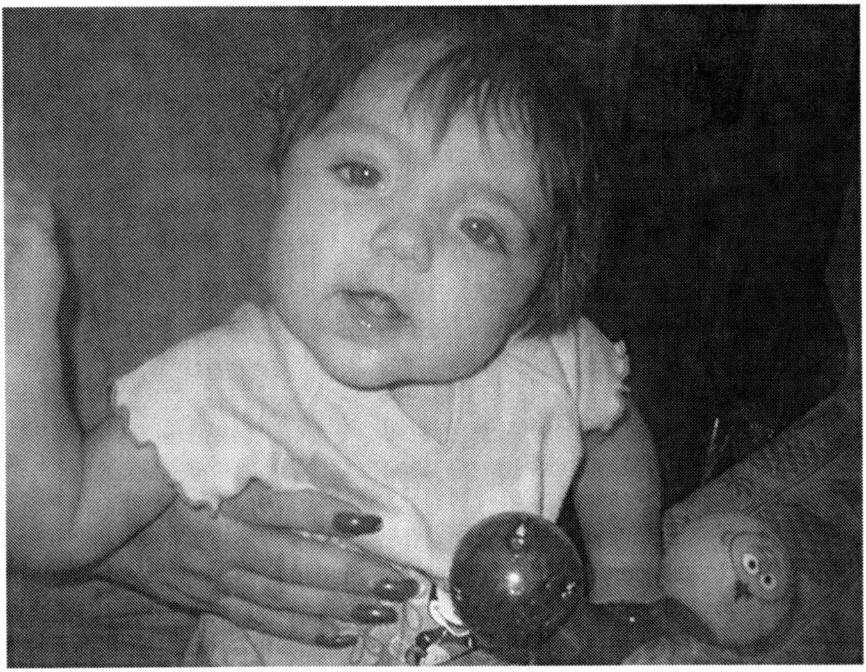

A Poem for Amber

There once was a princess and Amber was her name;
Conceived from a fire of love, she became the flame;
From the moment she was born, a flame she did start;
Warming everyone around, right down to the heart;
When you are in her presence it is very easy to see;
Why people come from near and far away,
just to be with thee;
With an innocent look and a great big smile;
Family miss her dearly from many a mile;
She is a princess that was sent,
From Heaven up above;
Warming everyone she meets,
With her flame of love.

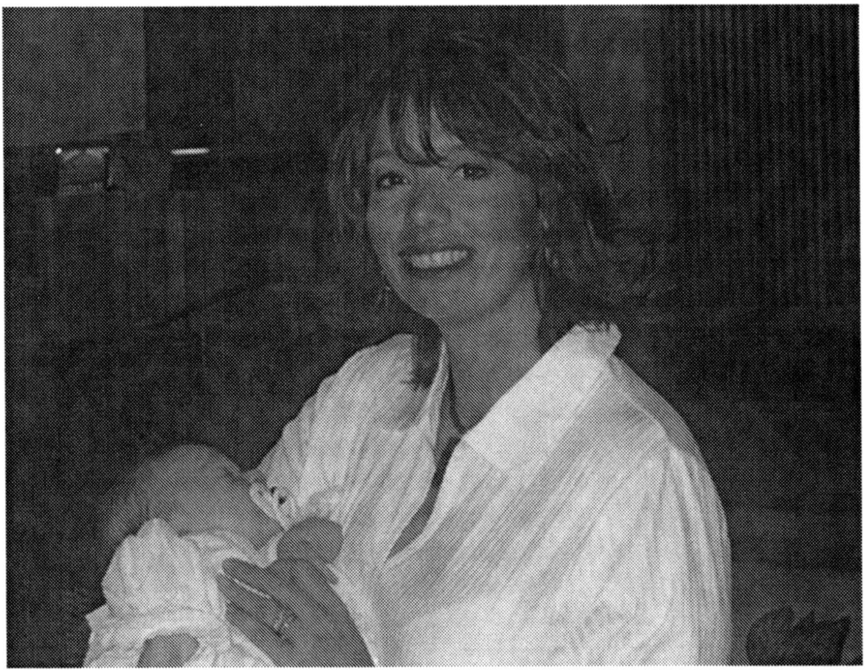

Gretchen's Poem

A mother and a baby start life out as one;
This bond stays true even when the baby
Comes out into the sun;

The love you feel now,
forever you will share;
Know each good time and bad time
Each other will be there;

The love for your child is like a rubber band;
It will stretch to the limits and snap back again;

The secret to it is let it stretch when it needs to,
But never enough to break;
And greeting it with open arms,
when a snap back it does make;

The future is unwritten,
except for the part;
Your child Now and Always will be,
A big part of your heart.

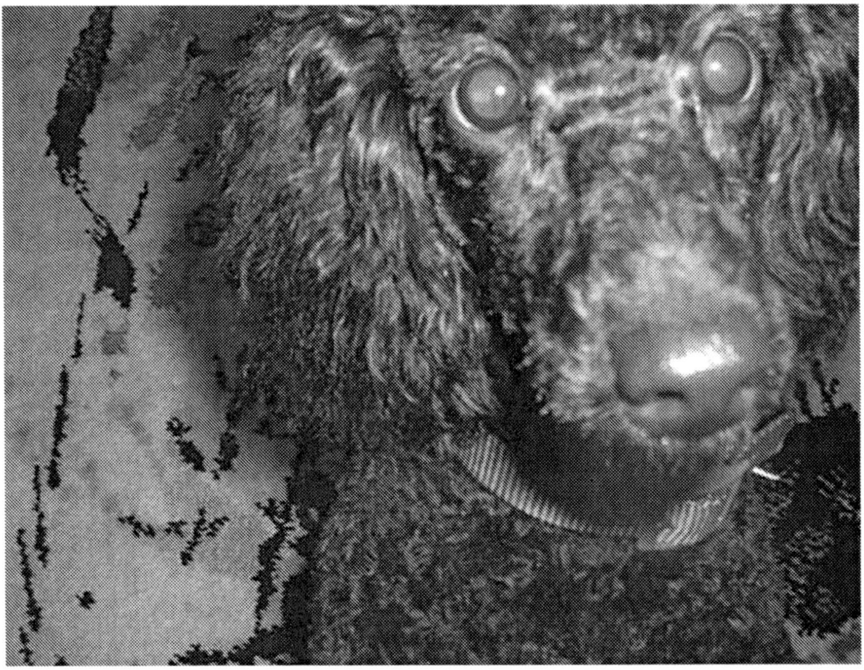

My Dog Brodie

For five whole months he sat in a cage in a store waiting to be bought;
Each day, losing a little more hope for the home he did sought;
Each week I went to visit, and I would pray to the lord;
To find him a home, because we could not afford;
Each week I would watch as the price came down;
Thinking each day a home he surely had found;
Every time I would return to still find him in that cage;
Leaving very sad at the level of my wage;
One day, I put together a plan, using extra money I make on the side;
I would give them a down payment and let them decide;
We went for our weekly visit, so out of his cage he did roam;
They took my down payment and that is how he got his new home.

I wrote this the day I had my dog neutered
From Brodie's point of view
I woke up this morning and my master I did see;
He was hanging his head low and looking very funny at me;
He grabbed my leash, to walk to a tree;
Which turned out so nice because I had to go pee;
On the way back from our walk he stopped at the car;
I jumped into the passenger's seat thinking we wouldn't go far;
He drove me to a building and we sat in a chair;
The room was full of dogs I think it was a fair; My Master took me into a room and I got a shot;
Everything after that, I have totally forgot;
When I woke up from my nap, I saw I had some cuts;
That's when, I sudden realized I was missing my nuts.

A Hero

He flew through the air as the man of steel;
Being Super Man on TV gave him quite appeal;
He saved the planet and so must more;
Protecting us from villains like Lex Luthur;
Then came the day of great tragedy.
When he fell from a horse for everyone to see;
The fall was so bad he couldn't even talk;
Once flying through the air, now he can't even walk;
Such an event would have brought most people down;
Instead this event gave him a crown;
He became Super Man for people just like him;
Fighting every day even though his chances was slim;
Fighting politics for people with problems just like his;
Using the influence he had earned in show biz;
He fought each battle, each and every day;
Until his condition finally took him away;
He showed what a super man is like off TV;
Fighting for rights for you and me;
Showing what a man can really achieve;
My hero of course is Christopher Reeve.

My Eulogy

If you are hearing this poem I would like to say;
It sounds like I finally had a bad day;
Every one of them has been great, up to the day before;
The last one wasn't so great need I say more;
I wasn't such a success in my life monetarily;
But most of you know that was never important to me;
My life was full of love and every day I would feel;
Too bad I can't leave you that in my will;
I promise to quit smoking for this you have won;
Well, I promise to quit right after my cremation;
This is a day for celebration not to be sad;
You're not really losing a friend, husband or dad;
You will not have to miss me from what I can see;
I will be with you always each time you think of me;
"A genius is never appreciated in his own lifetime,"
I have heard said;
Well, you know what you have to do,
now that I am dead;
I would like to leave you with these words of wisdom;
Take it to heart even though it might sound silly to some;
Live each day as if it was your last;
For me as you can see that time has passed;
Always show affection to everyone, no matter who they are;
Because all that affection will come back to you,
from near and far;
The love that you get, is equal to the love that you give;
If you want happiness in your life,
happiness you must live;
If you are crying when you hear this, for this I say hush;
I will see you in heaven,
but there is no need to rush.

Snail Man

I was having a nice drive and I was on my way to work;
When I came across a slow-moving car, thinking it was a jerk;
I thought I would go around, with no big deal;
Until I saw the hairy knuckles, wrapped around the steering wheel;
Looking into the car I could not see a head;
I didn't want to pass him for fear of being dead;
He was taking his Sunday drive, thinking speed is a crime;
He always leaves on Wednesday, so he can get to Sunday on time;
He always drives slowly, as careful as can be;
He hasn't driven over 20, since his model T.;
Sitting in his car, he can barely see over the Dash;
Only his slow speed keeps him from a crash;
He always ignores traffic sign, driving in a daze;
Saying they have added too many signs, since his buggy days;
Being caught behind him, time seems to stand still;
I'd like to pull out a rocket launcher and target in the kill;
I'd like to push him forward for the speed that he does lack;
If we would reach 40, he would die of a heart attack;
Drive slowly to his death, I think is his plan;
Until he actually dies, his is the **Snail Man.**

Flying Reindeer

Deep in the woods where no human would go;
Lived a herd of deer, some bucks and a doe;
The leader of the herd was a buck named Biff;
They were grazing on a mountain, right next to a cliff;
When next to them in the woods, arose such a clatter;
Biff stood to attention to see what was the matter;
He ran toward the noise with his eyes full of red;
Then slowly walked back and said, it's just a butthead;
Out from the woods walked two young bucks;
Who were alone in the woods and each down on their lucks;
They weren't to bright which was easy to see;
Walking toward Biff one tripped on a tree;
We are two brothers that have lost their way;
We were looking for a herd that would allow us to stay;
After looking them over Biff said,
you each have a spot on the back of your ear;
This is a magic spot found only on flying Reindeer;
They said, "We jump all the time and never could fly;
Biff said, It only works for first time if you are high in the sky;
Biff walk back to the herd and
told them I think they are on Meth;
As the brothers ran to the edge and jumped to their death.

The Poet's Stage

Somewhere out in cyber space is a place that few are aware;
A great place of truths, where a poet can share;
The poets that have found it, call it a home;
Always coming back to it, no matter where they roam;
This is a place where, your heart you can show;
Saying it, in words for everyone to know;
Each poem that we write we place in trust;
Knowing each time we post, we post a little piece of us;
Each new poet we do welcome with open hearts;
Knowing they have a home, when life throws its darts;
Everyone is welcome no matter what the age;
This place we call home is upon the Poet's Stage.

Spring

There is a special time of the year, when the birds start to sing;
When children outside playing becomes a familiar ring;
The trees sprout their leaves and the grass begins to grow;
Leaving in its past the winter, cold and the snow;
Walking in the grass with your bare feet;
Always looking in front of you, for some doggies treat;

The flowers fill the air with their magical smell;
You walk around light headed as if you were under spell;
The sun warms your body and then warms your soul;
Giving it back to you, healed from harsh winter's toll;
Of all the many magical wonders, the best I do know;
Is Mini skirts and bikinis and skin that girls show.

See I can be deep and shallow all at the same time.

The Easter Bunny

I gathered my equipment because I know the time is near;
I come up with a different plan, each and every year;

At dusk I shut my windows and always lock my door;
But every Easter Morning the Evidence is on the floor;

He used to bring me candy and hide a bunch of eggs;
Now he leaves his droppings, I slipped and broke both my legs;

It started at the age of eight, in my bare feet;
I accidentally left him exlax for his nightly treat.

Each year I have a shotgun and try to stay alive;
Because he always comes to visit, even at age of forty-five.

Each year waiting up late, I always fall asleep;
That's when he leaves his presents right at my feet;

I know you might be laughing, but this isn't very funny;
Advice to all the kids, do not piss off the Easter Bunny!

Ode to a Cockroach

Each night in my kitchen there is a party, you see;
I am just glad, they always forget to invite me;

Their music is so loud it keeps me awake;
Drinking spill beer on my counter and getting half baked;

Every once in a while, one will end up in bed with me;
Drunk cockroaches, get a little too friendly;

The poison I bought, it must be like speed;
After a night full of partying, some had OD'ed;

Most go sleep it off during the course of the day;
So once the lights go out they can come out and play.

Rebecca

With family comes drama, as most of you know;
Sometimes, pettiness and anger is the face it will show;

The people you call family are there from the start;
It is not like you can buy them at a local Walmart;

Walmart doesn't carry family, because it would not be fun;
To have customers returning product and wanting a refund;

With all of the drama and always getting lip;
All this because, I can't find my stupid sales slip;

Here is something that I would like to see;
A family member with a 20-year warranty;

What I suggest might seem quite odd;
But it would be official if issued by God;

When things seem so bad and bodies lay in the wake;
I have a safe haven, for my mind and soul to take;

To have an oasis, in this land of Mecca;
This is why I love my sister Rebecca.

Harry the Troll

Once Upon a time, in a land far, far away;
Lived a troll named Harry, who lived across the way;

He lived under a bridge and stopped everyone that passed;
Telling them the toll for crossing the bridge was to kiss his ass;

Everyone in the village and far as you can see;
Was starving in their homes, because no one would pay the fee;

One day a Knight rode into the village with Armor made of steel;
Seeing the starving village and wanting it to heal;

They told him of the troll who would not let them pass;
He said "I will save the village and kiss the troll's ass!"

The Knight rode to the bridge and was back in no time flat;
The village then ask, "Did you kill the troll?"

the Knight said, "Didn't think of that!"

Printed in the United States
101539LV00004B/624/A